Animals of Africa
ELEPHANTS

by Christy Mihaly

FOCUS
READERS

FOCUS READERS

www.focusreaders.com

Focus Readers is distributed by North Star Editions:
sales@northstareditions.com | 888-417-0195

Produced for Focus Readers by Red Line Editorial.

Photographs ©: Volodymyr Burdiak/Shutterstock Images, cover, 1; Windzepher/
iStockphoto, 4–5; Red Line Editorial, 6; OceanImpressions/Shutterstock Images, 9; Licinia
Machado/Shutterstock Images, 10–11; zahorec/Shutterstock Images, 12; Mogens Trolle/
Shutterstock Images, 14; Krishna Utkarsh Pandit/Shutterstock Images, 16–17; Taalvi/
iStockphoto, 19; WilcoUK/Shutterstock Images, 21; GomezDavid/iStockphoto, 22; Four
Oaks/Shutterstock Images, 24 (top); Claudia Paulussen/Shutterstock Images, 24 (bottom
left); Johan Swanepoel/Shutterstock Images, 24 (bottom right), 29; Brenda Smith DVM/
Shutterstock Images, 26

ISBN
978-1-63517-261-4 (hardcover)
978-1-63517-326-0 (paperback)
978-1-63517-456-4 (ebook pdf)
978-1-63517-391-8 (hosted ebook)

Library of Congress Control Number: 2017935142

Printed in the United States of America
Mankato, MN
June, 2017

About the Author

Christy Mihaly writes about animals, nature, science, history, and geography. She studied environmental science and has published books, articles, stories, and poems for readers of all ages. Her favorite childhood toy was a stuffed elephant.

TABLE OF CONTENTS

CHAPTER 1

ELEPHANT COUNTRY

An elephant **calf** is stuck in a water hole. The bank is too slippery. Two adult elephants go in. They push the calf up the side. The adult elephants touch the calf with their trunks. They have rescued him.

An elephant calf is comforted by its mother.

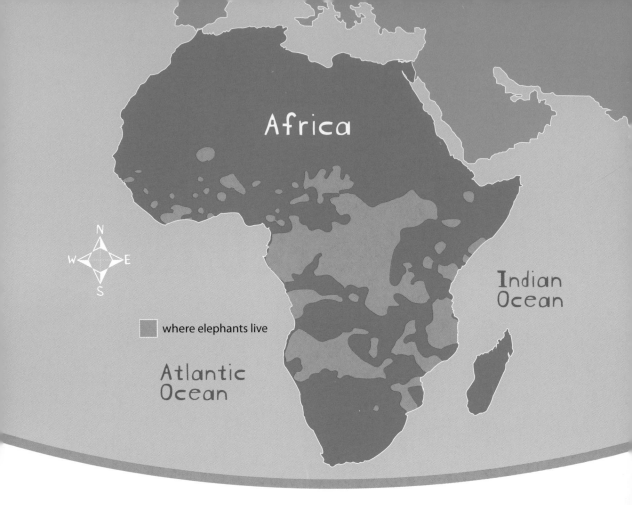

Africa

Indian
Ocean

where elephants live

Atlantic
Ocean

 Elephants live in many different areas of Africa.

African elephants roam more than 30 countries in Africa. They live in many **habitats**. They can be in forests, grasslands, and swamps.

There are two types of African elephants. Bush elephants live on the **savanna**. The sun is hot. Sometimes these elephants must travel far to find enough food and water. They use the **sparse** trees for shade on their journey.

Forest elephants stay mainly in thick **rainforests**. They are smaller than bush elephants. But they still leave wide paths between the trees when they walk.

HOW DO ELEPHANTS SAY HELLO?

Elephants can make at least 70 different sounds. They use these sounds to communicate. Some sounds are snorts and squeaks. Others are roars and special greeting calls. For exciting events, they trumpet loud and long. They might do this when a calf is born.

Elephants can hear others calling from more than 1 mile (1.6 km) away. They sometimes rumble so low that humans cannot hear the sound. Their rumbles vibrate through the ground. Far-off elephants feel the rumble through their feet.

An elephant makes a loud trumpet call.

Elephants also communicate with their bodies. They hold their ears and trunks in different positions. One position may be to say hello. Another position may mean it is time to leave.

CHAPTER 2

THE LARGEST ON LAND

Bush elephants are Earth's largest land animals. Adult bush elephants stand 10.5 feet (3.2 meters) tall at the shoulders. **Bulls** can weigh 14,000 pounds (6,350 kg). That is heavier than two pickup trucks.

 Bush elephant bulls are massive.

Forest elephants' smaller size lets them walk through wooded areas more easily.

Forest elephants are smaller.

They are 7.5 feet (2.3 m) tall.

They can weigh up to 10,000 pounds (4,500 kg).

Most elephants have two long **tusks.** Both females and males can have tusks. But some elephants never grow them. Forest elephants have tusks that grow straight. A bush elephant's tusks curve outward.

FUN FACT

Elephant feet are padded with fat. This cushions the animal's great weight.

A bush elephant shows off its curved tusks and huge ears.

An elephant has a long nose. It is called a trunk. It has thousands of muscles. The tip of the trunk has two finger-like parts. An elephant uses them to grip things.

Elephants have huge ears. They are approximately 6 feet (1.8 m) long. Each ear is approximately 4.5 feet (1.4 m) across.

FUN FACT

The shape of a bush elephant's ear is similar to the shape of Africa.

CHAPTER 3

AMAZING ELEPHANTS

The savanna is hot. Elephants flap their huge ears. This makes a nice breeze. It also cools down blood inside the ears. The cool blood flows through the elephant's body. It cools down the elephant.

Flapping its ears helps an elephant lower its body temperature.

But an elephant has other ways to keep itself cool. Elephants use their trunks. They suck gallons of water up into their trunks. They pour the water from their trunks into their mouths to drink. They also spray it over their bodies. It works like a cooling shower. Sometimes they

FUN FACT

When threatened, elephants spread out their ears. This makes them appear several feet wider.

PARTS OF A BUSH ELEPHANT

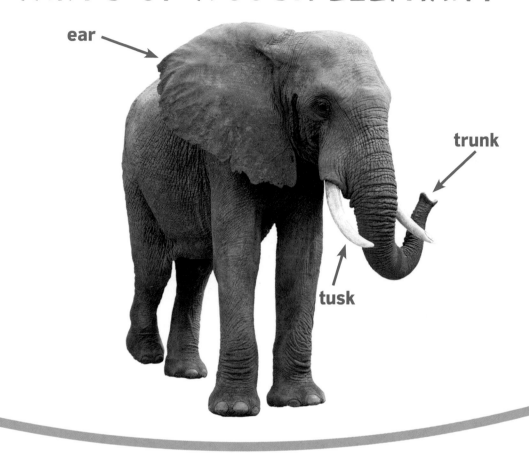

ear

trunk

tusk

suck up dust with their trunks. They spray the dust onto their skin. This protects their skin from the sun.

An elephant can use its trunk as a **snorkel**. The animal can breathe with its head underwater.

An elephant's trunk and tusks can help it eat. The trunk can grab things. It grasps food. Elephants dig for food and water with their tusks. However, they also use their tusks to defend their **herd**.

 An elephant can use its trunk to reach high leaves.

CHAPTER 4

AN ELEPHANT'S LIFE

Female elephants usually have one calf at a time. The baby weighs approximately 200 pounds (90 kg). It lives with its mother in a herd. A **matriarch** leads the herd.

Calves cannot fully control their trunks. They often trip over them.

ELEPHANT LIFE CYCLE

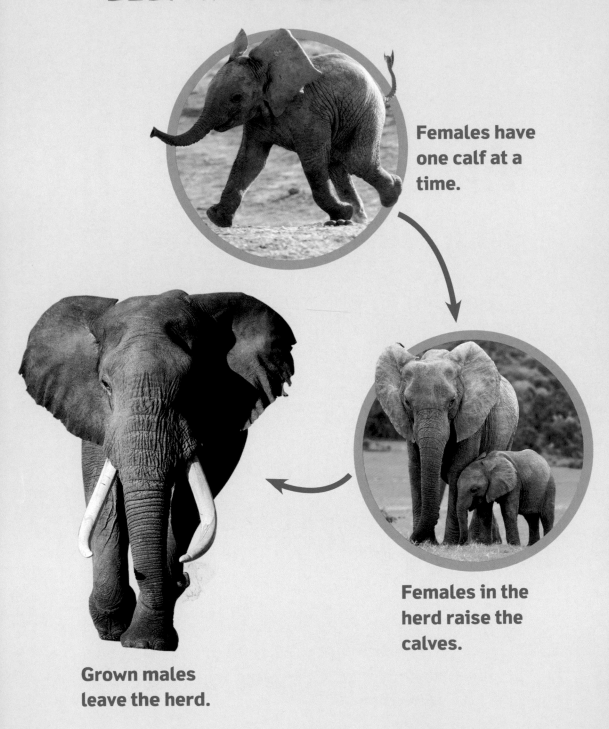

Females have one calf at a time.

Females in the herd raise the calves.

Grown males leave the herd.

24

The herd also includes other females and their calves. Everyone helps in a herd. All the females in a herd help to raise the calves.

Male elephants leave the family. This usually happens when they are approximately 14 years old. Adult bulls usually live alone.

FUN FACT

Elephants have great memories. They can recognize other elephants after years of separation.

 An elephant uses its trunk to eat leaves from a tree.

Elephants spend most of their time looking for food and water. Under the hot sun, they must travel long distances to find it.

These animals need a lot of food. In one day, an elephant can eat up to 300 pounds (136 kg) of food. Elephants often eat grasses and roots. They also eat fruit and bark. They drink 25 to 50 gallons (95 to 189 L) of water, too. An elephant can live to be 70 years old.

FOCUS ON
ELEPHANTS

Write your answers on a separate piece of paper.

1. Write a letter to a friend describing the main ideas of Chapter 3.

2. Would you like to see elephants in the wild? Why or why not?

3. Which African elephants can have tusks?
    A. both males and females
    B. only females
    C. only males

4. Why might an elephant spread out its ears when faced by a predator?
    A. The ears work as a shield.
    B. The ears can harm predators.
    C. The ears make elephants look scary.

5. What does **bank** mean in this book?

*The **bank** is too slippery. Two adult elephants go in. They push the calf up the side.*

   A. the bottom of a pond
   B. the side of a water hole
   C. the depth of a lake

6. What does **grasps** mean in this book?

*The trunk can grab things. It **grasps** food.*

   A. holds
   B. understands
   C. climbs

Answer key on page 32.

GLOSSARY

bulls
Male elephants.

calf
A baby or young elephant.

habitats
The type of places where plants or animals normally grow or live.

herd
A group of animals that stays together.

matriarch
An older female leader.

rainforests
Areas with thick stands of tall trees and plenty of rainfall.

savanna
A grassland with few or no trees.

snorkel
A tube that sticks up above the water level, allowing a swimmer to breathe while his or her head is underwater.

sparse
Few and scattered.

tusks
Long, pointed teeth that stick out from the faces of some animals.

TO LEARN MORE

BOOKS

Hibbert, Clare. *Elephant Orphans*. New York: PowerKids Press, 2015.

Hirsch, Rebecca E. *African Elephants: Massive Tusked Mammals*. Minneapolis: Lerner Publications, 2015.

Marsico, Katie. *Elephants Have Trunks*. Ann Arbor, MI: Cherry Lake Publishing, 2014.

NOTE TO EDUCATORS

Visit **www.focusreaders.com** to find lesson plans, activities, links, and other resources related to this title.

INDEX

Answer Key: 1. Answers will vary; **2.** Answers will vary; **3.** A; **4.** C; **5.** B; **6.** A